BREAKING LIGHT

Poems

by

Jane Lazarre

Hamilton Stone Editions

Copyright 2021
Jane Lazarre

Library of Congress Cataloging-in-Publication Data

Names: Lazarre, Jane, author.
Title: Breaking light / Jane Lazarre.
Description: Maplewood, New Jersey : Hamilton Stone Editions, [2021] |
   Summary: "Breaking Light is a volume of poetry whose many themes include elegies, prose poems, poems about illness, recovery, loss, lifelong friendship and love. Forms include sestina, villanelle and free verse. Introduction is by Professor Miryam Sivan of the University of Haifa where she teaches American Literature"-- Provided by publisher.
Identifiers: LCCN 2021001357 | ISBN 9780990376781 (paperback)
Subjects: LCGFT: Poetry.
Classification: LCC PS3562.A975 B74 2021 | DDC 811/.54--dc23
LC record available at https://lccn.loc.gov/2021001357

Editions

Hamilton Stone Editions
Maplewood, NJ 07040
www.hamiltonstone.org

BREAKING LIGHT

PREVIOUS WORKS BY JANE LAZARRE

The Communist and The Communist's Daughter

Inheritance, a novel

Wet Earth and Dreams, A Narrative of Grief and Recovery

Some Place Quite Unknown, a novel

Beyond the Whiteness of Whiteness: Memoir of a White Mother of Black Sons

Worlds Beyond My Control, a novel

The Powers of Charlotte, a novel

Some Kind of Innocence, a novel

On Loving Men, essays

The Mother Knot, a memoir

For Douglas, Adam, and Khary,
whose voices are cherished and beloved.

"Poetry (here I hear myself loudest)
Is the human voice,

and are we not of interest to each other?"
Elizabeth Alexander
Ars Poetica # 100: I Believe

CONTENTS

Introduction–Miryam Sivan 17
Virus Time, A Woman's Lament 23

I

Chiaroscuro 28
Vocabulary of Dreams 29
Civil Wars 33
Exposure 36
Childhood, Mohegan Lake 37
Imperfect Sestina 38
Post Reunion 39
Christmas 40
Country Dreams 41
Clashing Dreamscapes 43
Elegy for My Mother 46
Transferences 49
Thinking and Feeling 52
A Villanelle 54
Watching Children Play in the Muddy Bay 55
Firebirds 56

II

Metaphors 58
Schubert Sinking In 60
September Sketch 65
Wanting Silence 66
Floods and Drains 67
Writing During CT Scan Number 20 77

III

Family Portrait, a Cycle	80
Vincere (To Win)	80
Arm Over Arm	86
Shape Changes	91

IV

Music and Words	96
Like a Door Opening	97
Once White in America	98
Birth	100
The Sanctuary of Words	101
Passing Seventy	103
Remembering the Queen Mary and Seeing it in Long Beach Harbor with Aiyana Grace	104

Dedications for Individual Poems	107
Notes	109
Acknowledgements	111
Praise for Previous Work	113
Author's Biography	117

INTRODUCTION

Breaking Light is divided into four distinct yet resonant sections that weave together themes of light, death, dreams, and power. Rich lyrical lines, echoes and associations, insights and images, and recurring scenes of nature, are what Jane Lazarre uses to create a distinct poetic voice that simultaneously confronts and is humbled by the challenges of the human experience.

Light, in all its many wonderous literal and metaphorical manifestations, fills the pages of this collection. In the very first poem, a kind of preamble outside the formal four sections, "Virus Time, A Woman's Lament," in its very first sentence, Lazarre writes how the "sun is out/ more than in. Our fractured time leaps forward/ an hour moving in a minute into early night." Breaking light in these lines, as in many of the poems, does not only reference the beginning or ending of the light of day, but expresses the pressures that risk breaking the 'light,' the spirit of love, hope, and optimism, inside each of us.

The fluidity felt in the light and dark motif is reinforced by the many descriptions of bodies of water, and the experience of being inside and beside them. Water inspires serenity and awareness, which includes the necessity for both light and its absence. Along with the 'hope' of dawn, healing, and cyclicality of life, there are shadows of destruction that highlight pain and unkindness in our complicated world.

"Breaking light" can also be read as a reference for death. The recurring central loss of a mother's death in these poems is tracked by other losses that ripple out from it. Morning, and its homonym, mourning, break into light. Morning's birth contains loss and mourning of life itself. The poems' speakers sometimes identified as women, mothers, grandmothers, partners to men, often use an elegiac tone as they reckon with the 'remaining light.' The acuteness of what has passed, of what is no longer accessible, is not dimmed with time but is accentuated with age.

Dreamscapes and their surrealistic landscapes that settle right alongside hard realities are another central motif in the collection. The probing observant voice here is self-aware, sometimes even self-mocking, but mostly self-conscious about the world of suffering that humans move through from childhood until death. In "Vocabulary of Dreams," the speaker wonders: "Will nothing remain literal, even outside of dreams?" Dreams are the movies screened in the brain during sleep, but also the wishes, desires, and need for less cruelty, more healing, in a human world filled with injustices. These are dreams not easily put aside, those of a personal nature, nor those for our world:

"I am amazed by the longevity of longing,/ its persistent echoing colors/ dreamed in country dreams," the speaker reflects in "Country Dreams."

The poems develop from the grand facts of light and landscape, internal and external consciousness, to issues of power where the politics of personal choices, including love, resist social and political prejudices. In "Civil Wars" the speaker acknowledges that "we must risk terror,/ push past heroism, fear,/past stoicism, past false cheer,/not cover over/not move on/nor let go so fast/of what is going/or is gone." All this while ambivalences abound. To travel back into time, to touch the wounds, to feel the pain, anger and rivalry, to make memory manifest is not a simple task. And since color is wavelengths of light, colors and the values we imbue them with, come to include intimations of racism and its dangers. This is another view of 'breaking light.' To challenge definitions, to reach over gaps, to mend that which is 'broken' in a race defined society. Defiantly, in "Once White in America" Lazarre writes about "a woman who loves color and knows terror/ and hopes words might be/ the way to everything." And she is more specific, using the colors brown and black to describe loved human bodies. In "Schubert Sinking In", the poet expresses relief when "[m]y sons, young Black men whose beautiful jaw lines and soft lips, whose gentle eyes and minds [...] have returned to their homes safely tonight." In "Birth" physical descriptions of a second son, specifically his "darkening" skin and eyes, converge with the collection's nature descriptions, where by default, brown is a ubiquitous and healing color: tree trunks and branches, falling leaves, and most importantly, nurturing sustaining earth itself.

With time, with age, the poet comes to gracefully accept the narrowing of the frame of influence – yet despite diminishment, there is power and the holding fast to the truth in love and connection. In "Post Reunion," the speaker reconciles with the changes, and plays on the word light, in another turning, to mean the lessening of weight. "Unfettered by love or rage/ Lighter and lighter/ I feel my age. I will work less./ I will lie down more, relish the quiet, the dark." She will bring herself to a hard-earned and not so easily understood repose. And in "Wanting Silence," the darkness, like in the previously cited poem, is akin to silence. This is not non-communication, but a kind of softness that allows consciousness to look deeper into the self, to reach for clarity, to touch critical insights.

In a prose-poem section of the long piece, "Floods and Drains," the speaker says: "When I was a girl I was a painter, and then I was a young woman and I became a writer. Now I fear I have missed my calling. Words come to me in images. Moods in colors. If I were to paint this story, instead of writing myself into and out of prison through the painful grace of words, I could perhaps move with less careful intention. I might be able to touch, unaware of course, that process we call primary." Much as we, along with Lazarre, draw on primal images, we also draw on primal sounds, or words, to create meaning and beauty in our baffling world. Robert Pinksy wrote: "Poetry connects us with our deep roots, our evolution as an animal that evolved rhythmic language as a means of transmitting vital information across the generations. We need the comfort and stimulation that this vital part of us gets from the ancient art."

There is a formality in these pages, a reliance on structure to contain the poetry's powerful yet often restrained emotions. The carefully drawn descriptions of light, nature, mourning, and love are images that provide a deep and familiar 'comfort and stimulation' that remain with us long after we've stopped reading.

Dr. Miryam Sivan
University of Haifa, Israel

These poems were written before 2020, the year of the COVID-19 pandemic, the fears and rage of the Trump years, and the rise of Black Lives Matter. I am therefore inserting a brief writer's preface in the form of a poem written when the virus was at its height in New York City, then the epicenter of the pandemic and the place where I live.

And I am including a second dedication of this collection:

To all the heroic workers at The Brotherhood Sister Sol, a non-profit organization in Harlem, New York: To all the staff and leadership who have labored to feed the hungry every Wednesday, while continuing the ongoing struggle for social justice and supporting the young members, their families and the community in every possible way.

Salud, y (one of these days) Victoria.
Words written by poet, Edwin Rolfe, in Madrid, Spain, 1936, to Bill Lazarre, my father.

Virus Time, A Woman's Lament

All I seem to want to do is draw trees, leafless
delicate winter trees, bare though sun is out
more than in. Our fractured time leaps forward
an hour moving in a minute into early night.
We saw tiny buds of pink
blossoms on three trees our last day out.

Now we stay in, sometimes a careful walk
down the block, around and around until
our phones tell us: one mile.
We count the days with breaking tender hope
longing for peace, relief from fear of infection,
that our suddenly unsafe privileged selves will not
starve, homeless wanderers holding our crying children
to our thinning chests, like the millions
moving across this long-endangered earth of ours.

Strong men – the name for dictators, autocrats
and tyrants. The ones who led us here. *Strong men,*
arms held straight out in that ancient nightmare salute,
leading us into war and pestilence.
The numbers of the poisoned dead reach higher now
than those tiny petals on the budding trees.

Our fears grow with spring, our rage explodes,
a sudden flowering first on the east side of Manhattan,
bare and blossoming trees lacing our view of the makeshift
military hospital and morgue on 105 Street,
a few blocks south from where my second son was born.
And we want justice, yes, we long
to turn our faces maskless to the spring
and coming summer sun, to embrace our grownup
sons and daughters, our grandchildren, our aging lonely friends,
protecting them with prison walls against desire.

Our fears grow with the spring until we feel the fires
and storm of hate in our dreams and aching shoulders,
in whispered confessions on the phone, even in our emails
confessing, we want to kill the *Strong Men* who
brought us here with their lies and unimaginable greed.

Leave us the tender loving quiet and the easy talking men,
the silent listening men, the brave resilient and fearful men
who love as women try to love, not always brave, not always
kind, trying to be mothers to ourselves, to our children, small
and grown, to our benighted earth, our endangered home.

Let there be mourning long and loud as New York City
shouts at seven each night, with claps and banging pots,
from terraces and window hidden faces, at times a slight
reflection glimpsed. We hear for ten full minutes,
in every part of town, the drums of gratitude to Front Line
Workers, those brave men and women fighting this war
with its mounting dead and wounded. I will not call them soldiers.
I will call them Mother Men and Mother Women
bringing food to stores and doors, who heal the sick or watch
the dying die, wrapping them in blue
and guiding them on moving beds to temporary rest,
drivers of ambulances and fire engines,
all other traffic suddenly spare or gone, racing to hospitals
of canvas and stone or ice filled morgues.
Let there be mourning.

I loved to wake you in the morning child, my fingers stroking
your cheeks, kissing eyelids from a shallow sleep. Time
to wake now darling. Or touching you father, that last time,
your skin already turned death-cold. I love
to touch your hair dear husband and companion, stroking
in a slow caress, my fingers in your hair
become your fingers in my hair. We touch our thinning hair
with love and fear of loss we could not bear. I touch my scars,
my wrinkled skin, my deepest memories.

Grief is buried with fear, fear is buried with anger,
anger is buried with our grief again, circling
like the blocks we circle, vigilant and masked,
watchful of someone we might have greeted smiling once.

Now we are wary of coming too close. Come close
to me beloved, I used to whisper. Let me hold you.
Now I count the days of lost touching, of buds falling
into pinkwhite pillows on the ground, edges slowly turning brown.
I count the days with memories of your soft young
eyelids sons, your grandfather's cold forehead.

And you, granddaughter, nieces - I feel in my fingers your
thick hair black and brown. Your small straight back
when we played the blanket game. How you kissed
your mother's eyelids. *Her favorite color
was burnt orange*, you wrote on a special card.
Your once long and thick black hair tied back
as you organized my terrace pots. Your faces, black and brown
and tan and blossom pink, Jewish African and Italian faces,
like old country photographs, family features shadows now.

I am drawing branches. They reach to the edge of the page
as they break into smaller and smaller parts, still bare
though even walking in the park that last time I saw
a line of trees with delicate, not-yet-flowering buds
hard and firm and comforting to the touch.

I remember my hand laid on your cheek,
your hand. All I seem to want to do
is touch your hand.

April, 2020

Remember, we don't love like the flowers, from a single
Year only; when we love arises in our arms
The sap from immemorial ages ...
    Rainer Maria Rilke, "The Third Elegy,"
    Duino Elegies

I feel that poetry is essentially elegiac in nature.
    Maxine Kumin, *Always Beginning*

I

Chiaroscuro

I dream of light
in darkness
a darkened
light
or a light too white
to see
it's not the dark
of night
but of earliest morning
just before dawn
like waking in November
(I must have said out loud)
my own voice waking me
a time of saving daylight
the month when I was born
(I heard my own surprise.)

It was a cold dark November
morning
breaking slowly into light.

Vocabulary of Dreams

Double meanings, paradoxes everywhere:
curtains, screens and veils,
like the archway
curved
between living and dining room
in my childhood home
a wall that stood between
myself and them, and seemed
to keep me out.
Behind the dream screens –
as intangible and likely to disperse
into a merely dimming light
as in the open archway
when they ate together every night -
I often see, when looking to the side,
the real thing, the very thing itself
as if in a circle of light.

A crowded room signifying loneliness.
A former friend,
selfish and mean, calls me on the phone -
but the voice feels familiar, suffused
with the sound of my own.
A wedding - but even in language-slips
funeral and *wedding* get confused.
Repeated taxi rides, the drivers always
foreign, inscrutable, hidden from view -
racist imagery, or merely unknown?
One of my dream versions of you.

And what shall I call you?
I like soul doctor, or spirit doctor,
so I can hold on tight
to certain slivers of knowledge,
sunk in deep intuitive whirls of knowledge
I feel with your face out of sight.
And double meanings recur:
the *docks* at the edge of the city,
at least once a week, the *sea* –
last night it was calm and bordered,

a long swimming pool sea,
simple and safe in swimming-pool-blue,
(you swim only in pools – you said,
the sea is too cold for you.)
The architecture of childhood:
An archway, and through its arc
a gleaming light,
and I am looking in.

Once I swam in the Russian
River, on the west coast of California.
I thought it was the rushin' river
until I was told no – the country,
named for the immigrants
who settled here.
Still, I kept dreaming it rushing,
and me, swept away from some home land,
emigrating somewhere from somewhere else.

Children are crying,
in danger of falling
in the middle of the street
of onrushing traffic.
Or they are laughing,
safe in my arms –
I've caught them in time –
boys and girls, black and white
and "mixies" –
(that's what some of
them call themselves,
a friend told me -
the ones from mixed
families like mine.)

A woman – her sad face scarred, and brown –
neither unfamiliar nor a female version
of my sons. She's mine. She's me.
I see her leaning toward me,
riding past in a bus,
happening by. When she fails
to come for many nights,
I look for her, I try to bring her in
and fail. I can't control the state I'm in.

The list of recurring images
goes on and on – like I
always wish the Causeway would,
the road between Orient Bay and Sound.
Instead, too soon we're past it,
on our way to town.

It's a narrow road.
Water on both sides
changing colors
with the light and tides.
The sky reflects it
in the morning -
both gray as if to welcome rain,
or the stunning blue of my father's eyes,
speckled here and there with white –
as plain as dawn. At twilight,
a rose stripe cracks
like sudden lightning,
and edges fade to purple until
the whole visible world
is purple so dark
it might as well be black.

Nearby, not in a dream, in life,
little girls listen to ritual words
on Shabbat – each Friday night.
A father feeling dense and rich
to me from tangled history.
A mother overwhelmed and open armed –
around her face, her cupped hands bend -
v'yishmerecha -
she speaks the Hebrew words I do not comprehend.

Our room faces water -
that same ever changing bay.
More than once each day
I walk part way around it
until a rock wall stops me.
There I stand and look across
at Shelter Island from the shore.
Then turning back, toward home,
I hear some version of those words,

v'yishmerecha and can't remember any more.

Shelter Island. A wall of rock. Words I partly understand.
Will nothing remain literal, even outside of dreams?
Must I always rush and fly, sucked
backward, then ahead,
unquiet and spinning,
lost in dense meaning,
and the meanings, when elusive
and disguised, fill me with dread.

I dream locked stairwells, always blue,
a country place – old and known,
yet new. A desperate wish to analyze -
my friend's translations of her prayer, options multiply.
May you be watched over
Or, may you be enveloped in
God's attention, or – in God's recognition.
I would fit myself with perfect comfort
into any of these pleas,
but once again I'm lost at sea,
or it's dark at the edge of the city.
The street is narrow, bordering the dock.
I'm far from home. It's night.

In the morning on the Causeway
I look out and breathe –
the sky, the sea, the grass,
the blue, the rain, the light,
and feel the meanings press me through
the archway - or so it sometimes seems
in the vocabulary of my dreams.

Civil Wars

1.
Ebb tide at Corn Hill
Bay – a strong wind
winding through my mind,

words and images
I'd rather store away in
notebooks or stories

changed enough
to veil if not fully hide
memories of my own

losses that become the faces of strangers,
refugees I know only from a tv screen, who walk
toward makeshift, crowded sandy homes.

We wander more than walk
down a silent empty effervescent beach
of low tide salty sand.

And you are wondering
a question, put to me,
as we meander by the sea,

where flood and ebb tides change topography
as dramatically as even distant wars
invade our lives, you say to me,

Why didn't I know my brother?
I hear an echo, another sister
speaks of buried wishes.

I wish I had known my brother,
she said, standing strangely still
in a garden of fuchsia flowers

cherry blossoms in April
behind the mausoleum –
I did not say

but wondered silently
do I know my sister?
for we have lived so far

apart so long, can we claim
to know a life, to sift
its joys from losses,

sorrows unrepaired from long unburied pain?
I would love to fix the broken parts,
say what I longed to say when we were girls,

but what is broken
may stay broken, in ourselves
and in the world.

2.
No longer can I dream or write
of the rescued world my father
believed to be as certain
as these changing tides.

Now, half a century past his death
Egyptian soldiers slaughter Muslim brothers
erasing even Syrian carnage from our
front pages, while I

am reading of post-war
Berlin – shattered buildings, shattered bodies
on storm-wrecked shores, even the idea of
wholeness drifts and drowns.

Yet now, the city is restored,
Germany leads the European Union
preaching austerity, while Greeks drown
and we believe in restitution,

as if the bloody parts
do not remain.
This week Egypt news is gone.
It's Syria again.

3.
It's flood tide now
narrowing a dampened lane
back up the beach, now single file,

your back is turned to me.
I know this back, its Yoga strengthened
spine, its shoulder curves,

so like your mother's and your daughter's,
and I have known your losses -
first your father, then your mother gone,

as now I know your torn
devoted love, a rip tide rising from a storm,
when last month your only brother died.

Witnesses or victims
of the pain, brothers
lost, sisters maimed,

bodies bloodied, spirits
shattered, broken backs
and faces turned away -

we must risk terror,
push past heroism, fear,
past stoicism, past false cheer,

not cover over
not move on

nor let go so fast
of what is going
or is gone.

Exposure

You know the one:
You're outside, at a meeting,
teaching a class, at a party having a drink
but you're naked, or half naked. You forgot
to put on your – whatever, whichever,
something essential,
something ordinary.

You remember the feeling:
A child called
into a room full of strangers,
say hello, dear,
but she's forgotten her clothes,
or she's made to change
into a dry suit on the beach,
only a flimsy, slipping towel
precariously draped.

She died of exposure.
The meaning lies in coldness,
a wind or water so cold it freezes
the insides, the body amputated
bit by frozen bit,
the skin's work
rendered useless, torn wrapping
on a secret gift.

This gift was once no secret.
I wanted it exposed.
But wasn't there a sturdy, silver wrap,
around a core of heat
that warmed like summer mist,
warding off paralysis?

Was my flesh less easily sliced,
bone less easily shattered?

Childhood, Mohegan Lake

Outside the ropes,
borders of the permissible
swimming area, the large quiet lake
stretched toward shores
we never visited. I don't recall
swimming across, not once
in all those summers.
Lily pads covered the surface
near our beach: green leaves embracing
their white flowers, glistening
petals spread open by the sun.
Grasses framed the shore line –
I picture them swaying in a never ending breeze –
and the bottom, like mud –
dark silt or clay – thick and soft.
You would sink way down.

On the wide lawn
we watched the boys
play baseball. Between innings
we necked beneath the trees.
Blankets strewn with soda bottles, chips –
We smoked.

Imperfect Sestina
for Mike Manoff

I knew you only as a little child,
a younger sibling in Mohegan's free
love family, a rare belonging
til then unknown to me, to you, Mike, and
to all of us. From even this place you
are gone, except perhaps surrounding all

the trees, the sky, the air, the rain, the breeze.
The children made a game we often played,
a play we all made up of knights and queens,
of castles, moats, of swords and kings and slaves.
We were the older ones, directors all,
and stars. You were a little kid and told

to play the tree, or be the air, we'd say,
laughing at our joke, our bossy age.
Now I hope you are the gentle air,
part of your spirit passing over us,
this grass, this lake, this old familiar house
with its big room where safety somehow spread

around us and within us, til we grew
old and away, but we return today
to find it all still here, the peace,
the sense of being free, of coming home.
We were ourselves, and found contentment in
this place. We leaned out toward the trees.

We came to mourn your too soon chosen death.
We turned our faces toward the lake, the sky,
the fields, the baseball diamond where you played,
and tried to hear your laugh without a care,
to see again your exceptional beautiful face,
and wonder why you felt you had to die.

And still, we hope to feel you in the air.
We long to glimpse you in the tree's green lace.
We'd gladly kneel, if that might part the sky.

Post Reunion

The trees are bare but not abandoned
I see a nest left over from summer.
A yellow balloon is tangled in a branch
Giving the illusion of light.

Short winter days lengthen
Minute by minute toward spring
And I love the slow movement. No one
Visits. You can walk for miles.

In the cold, I am finally spent
So I head home broke but not broken
Only penniless, empty, and slow
Wandering sadly in the park.

Unfettered by love or rage
Lighter and lighter
I feel my age. I will work less.
I will lie down more, relish the quiet, the dark.

Christmas

I inhale the pine aroma
of trees cut down to die
for our holiday pleasure.
They are lining the avenues,
some in full aromatic spread,
others tethered in white net
for carrying home.

In that quick inhalation
I feel the old spirit
when gifts for children
and children
filled the rooms, and
somehow my feet
remember to skip in
a sudden move down
Columbus Avenue.

The tree is lit,
the night comes early.
I am dark, and the tree doesn't smell much.
I have to press my face against the branches
to get a good whiff.
Later I am wandering
through unfamiliar neighborhoods,
trying to count lights instead of losses.
I dream of heading home.

Country Dreams
>after reading Rita Dove's *Mother Love*.
>"*No story is ever finished, it just goes
>on...*"

She is coming to me
more and more as I grow
older and older

I see her in green,
warm silvery grey, a touch of pink
in a flowered accessory,
dark mahoganies from Paris.
I was a girl, small and wild.

We don't believe in after-life
they said, but now she's here again
her brownblack hair – her skin
tanned olive brown - she must have been
in the country. Country dreams,
I call the dreams I dream of her.

Everyone said she was beautiful.
Everyone says that about dead mothers.
Was she? Who

cares, I only want to gaze
at this face I have longed for,
the years like a maze,
her hands reaching for
me? – she is kneeling

angry or loving,
no matter, we are gathering
Queen Anne's Lace, we are always near
a river, there are mirrors,
clear water, Violets,
Black Eyed Susans - then suddenly
the world,

the sky is cloudy, misty
in its drift and wave,
brown earth hills
deepen to purple, then begin to pale
until it's all pastel.

Even green and rosy pink
can fade, shimmer at the edges
like the last moment of a sunset,
where I appear to stand.

I am amazed by the longevity of longing,
its persistent echoing colors
dreamed in country dreams.

Clashing Dreamscapes

The interior
has always been
my business. I live inside.
Oh, I walk a lot.
Most women do,
and stretch and jump and lift
weights
in the gym.
I meet friends,
eat salads filled with
nutritious vegetables,
a little scrumptious cheese
on hard crusted bread.
But I live in here

With my long ago
child making up
stories, dressing
characters and decorating rooms,
like we used to do playing
with our paper dolls.
They were large rooms,
but they felt close
and breathless, so I began
staring out of windows
or into what we all called:
Space.

Somber rooms, haunted hallways
filled with gathering ghosts.
Not watery white ghosts –
rather the familiar dead.
Pale green rooms
with pale pink
blossoms, my mother's colors
left to me when she turned into
the leading ghost.

I walk the interior
not always cast as rooms -
long corridors may wind instead,
in a roaming light I've seen before
if not precisely home.
Still, when dead ghosts
are in, I go out.

I talk to
myself, on the street
pretending I am
on the phone.
Soon, loneliness and longing
drive me back within
to walk the corridors where I find
a place of shadow rooms,
my childhood home.

Lights dim -
deep grey, pigeon blue
and yellow nearly white -
then red fades into pink,
a liquefying green,
or unmixed contrasting colors
from the thick air
of that old time.

A place of warm thick quilts,
and threadbare sheets,
kitchens sometimes barren,
sometimes full of feasts.
A gleaming porcelain bath
beneath a row of orange flowered tiles
next to toilets full of shit.

An ancient strange hotel where I
sometimes live.
I wander through its
few or many rooms,
and find or don't find food.

There is the deep river
I have known from years of
interior walking.
I rush to its banks
dreaming in the dream
of a mesmerizing swim.
It is a night
of dangerous tides,
dark tempting bridges
too far above to climb.

There are buses going nowhere
then sudden arrivals
where the dead
surround me once again.

But on some lost nights
I see the fearful shapes,
what lurks, and I may find
a saving grace,
recall the place I need to be,
remember where I'm meant to go
and who I'm meant to be.
And if the moon is bright
I may see clearly
how to rescue sons,
husband, granddaughter, friend
from each impending doom.

That child is back again
as we grow old. Let us
take her in our arms this time,
caress her hair,
endure our fears,
embrace her in these
ancient rooms.

Elegy for My Mother

I have always written around her,
around and around and around.

I sing a chorus,
then you come in,
our voices harmonize,
frère Jacques, frère Jacques –
ding dang dong, ding dang dong.
A round, she said.
Around and around and around.

Old used memories repeated too often:
The white kotex, her breasts before they were removed,
lifting my sister's eyelid to remove a cinder from her eye.
   I'll be loving you always . . .
   Knock, knock, who's there?
   The white sheet, the shout:
   Be quiet!! The door closed silently.
   Screams in the night, my body tightly curled.
   Our mother's broken pearls.

On the merry-go-round
My father's face appearing, disappearing, reappearing.
The terror, each time I fly or gallop by the place he stands.
Across the space between the horses
I hold my baby sister's hand.
Around and around and around.

Your velvet collared suit, silk violets, chiffon scarf,
perfect elegant accessories
your presence, here then gone,
absorbed in grownup mysteries,
a professional woman with a Maiden Name,
the Queen Mary rose up like a ship of death
and took you to Paris, an early death to me.

"She had her breasts removed."
Said, like they were splinters, or old upholstery.
"Only sixty-nine pounds when she -"
The cut of a cut-throat murdering thief -
came in without a sound, when I was fast asleep.

I shaped a longing that would keep her around.
Around and around and around.

O, young woman only just past a girl,
This: your grandsons are older than you
ever got to be. I want to love you as if you
were not dead – faulted and ordinary.
Come, I'll hold you around, as your mother would have said,
come, die again, so I
can rock you, stroke your hair
I would hold you to my breasts –
oh – but they're no longer here,
removed, sliced off *– like yours –*
and even now, I –

Cannot remember her hard, flat chest.
Only a vague impression lingers.
There's a narrow ridge of bone
I trace across my chest at night.
Armpit to armpit – I slowly pull my finger
Like a moving pencil on a pad,
Or a chisel on a stone.

can I write you now? Can I write you
not around you? Can I zero in?

When she died they
Divided us up: an unwritten will.
I my mother's, she her father's child.
Our grownup children chastise us:
It was all those years ago, and *still?*
We carried on the anger
Like we were little girls.
Yet, I know I'm like our father,
And we both wear our mother's pearls,
Hers restrung on a long silk cord -
   the necklace was a choker,
   not in fashion any more -
Mine are long enough to
Circle round my head, as if
I were a bride, about to wed.

*Your crown of pearls, rough and real
pulled down across a bony chest
or strung on sturdy silk
the thread is pink
the jewels like milk.*

Transferences

When I met my mother
at the west side docks –
it was 67 years ago –
   Come on! I'm still there?
Come on with me, I'm still
there,
I met my mother
at my doc's. Tall
and graceful he
leaned over toward me, ruthless
at times, miraculously
kind. Many more than one
of a kind – a motherman,
a bus driver, a skeleton floating
just beneath the surface
of the water, an ancient
wooden dock.

And now you, a woman
in your radiant white
blouses. An exquisite
one today, embroidered with
interlocking circles of silver,
a chain of circles suggesting
infinite danger,
a thing that never ends.

You want to know about my mother?
Death is her name   a woman called Death
I said as a child smiling shouting weeping –
She's Dead, but Death is a prettier word –
her name is Death. I'll call her Death -
bitterness and hunger crossing paths.

On the west coast I sailed across
a sea where I saw the Queen Mary
anchored and docked,
too old to ride the waves
again – I was far
from the west side docks

where I shouted Good Morning
Mama! Look! My new white boots!
Ocean wind and rain drowned
out my small cry but she waved.
He wavered, I hoped,
between professional discipline
and uncontrollable love, shoot
countertransference to hell, death
to the discipline that saved me.

And he drove those buses for years
in my dreams – we were always lost.
Streetcars, my father
called old Philadelphia buses,
streetcars he learned to negotiate,
like me, longing to master
a new country.
A streetcar named
desire. My son playing
Stanley. My father jumping
on board, in his hand
an orange, tasted for the first time.
I feel the succulent juices
seeping through his fingers.

I wanted to taste you, I may
have dared to say
in a hesitant whisper wanting/
not wanting to be heard – I
want to eat you take
you inside me as I was
once inside of her, of Death,
to be inside of you Fatherman
Doctorman.

Now you're dead like them,
and I'm afraid of wanting Death again.
Come back. Come on
with me. I'm there again
I never called her
Mama, I write it clumsily even now
hitting wrong keys.
Mama, you called her, Mama,
you persisted

insisting on the lost word,
the buried plea.

I, always too dependent
on the kindness of strangers
complied and
I lay down for you.

*Make no mistake, new woman guide,
I see those old sea-rivers of guilt and rage,
and I'm afraid of falling into shadows,
ancient creatures lurking in long rotting
dismantled wooden docks.
Good morning ancient creatures,
my old dead alive again
in this new death, lost, lost again.*

Come on, come on, come on
with me into shadows take
my hand this writing hand –

No, leave me be
too old to ride the seas again
the radiant white
silver striped
infinite seas.

But yes, come with me again,
boldly over ancient waving seas again,
I see it's ancient mourning time again.

Thinking and Feeling

"As yet I had not thought. I had only listened, watched, dreaded;
now I regained the faculty of reflection." *Jane Eyre*

If I can only think, finally *think*
like that brave young girl, that other Jane,
wandering the darkest moors,
her journey not away
from him but toward herself,
to map and find a place for pain.

Years ago I walked
the blue-lit sanctuary at Chartres,
and heard the guide recount
how stories were embedded in
the glass of unique indigo.
So few could read, the pictures told the tale
of death and resurrection.
Imagine how miraculous
it must have seemed, how many
nights the faithful may have dreamed
their savior saving them from death.
Down those sacrosanct aisles
they crawled on knees
to show their faith.

I was a Jew in church, a Jew in Europe
carting history, hearing its percussion
loud and drumming in my ears:
the screaming mix of anguish
in the Memorial to the Jewish Dead;
the repulsion I always feel
beneath a crucifix; the dread
of invading armies marching
down the Champs-Élysées.

And yet, in Synagogue
I'm lonely too, aware
of all I don't believe,
of all, despite the background
of my father's soulful music
I don't and cannot share.

A stranger in the village – another story
of unbelonging, of outside looking in.
Baldwin's testimony
to his blackness; of the whiteness
that in Switzerland and Chartres
excluded him: *for this village –
is the west – the cathedral at Chartres
says something to them which it
cannot say to me – I am in Africa
watching conquerors arrive.*

Outsider looking in,
I wonder at the miracle of blue,
the stories pressed in glass,
I claim within me that magnificence
as I would a baroque string quartet,
or The Pietà in Rome –
a marble mother's arms outstretched –
and yes, I can imagine
the awesome emptiness left
by a dead son;
or my sister's healing vision of
our father's spirit resting
in Tomales Bay for all eternity,
three thousand miles from me.

I am excluded, yet *thinking* -
I can be a stranger and withstand
exclusion and the pain,
and for a blessed while
I am that other Jane.

A Villanelle

I try to think straight when my feelings grow
The spirit feels so real, the soul so deep,
I'm trying to remember what I know.

You find it hard to let your feelings show
You bury longing, even anger in your sleep.
I try to think straight when my feelings grow.

I hold you and speak softly, kiss your brow
I feel each limb, each bone I want to keep
Until slowly I remember what I know.

I've even whispered, will you sing it now?
And then you do, the song that makes me weep.
I try to think straight when my feelings grow.

This life gets hard, friends die, disease abounds.
I cannot lose you – I will sink in grief.
There'll be no point in anything I know.

Fear of death is here, it's all around.
Can souls still be together – a part to keep?
I try to think straight when my feelings grow,
Believe I know what I can never know.

Watching Children Play in the Muddy Bay

I remember when you
were three or even two

and tiny things enchanted
you - we lay in the yard and stared

into the grass, we pretended
the tiny stalks of green were dense forests

and tiny pebbles were explorers
creeping gingerly along their way

through the tall forests.
We did not make a move.

Our faces nearly touched, I kept up the story
of the dangerous journey of the brave tiny pebbles.

I touched your chin, pointed your
darling face in the direction of a spot of grassless earth.

Look - a clearing behind the trees, I said,
It will all end happily.

I kissed your head and lay my face against your hand.

Firebirds

A dark lake rolls like an ocean,
Or closer to a stormy bay, its waves
High but safer than the open sea.

I stand by the shore
And tell my daughter:
Cross the lake with your father.

But she is frightened and
No, Mother, she tells me,
Everyone knows Firebirds

Live in the lake and may rise up,
In flames at any moment,
I am afraid to go, my daughter says.

Just go with your father.
All will be well, it will be all right, I say.
The night is darkening to near opaque.

Still I say: Firebirds will not kill you
Girl, if only – what? I wonder,
If you are not afraid?

Steer your boat between them
So neither bird can light
On the rim of your small craft.

But they are such large birds,
Dancers dressed as birds,
Artists of the body, not of words.

I faced the dark stage then,
Wings I feared as a child,
Red stripes of fire and night.

The lake is dark and wild.
Her father stands in the bow.
They move into the night.

II

Metaphors

I am inside a small room,
the audiologist inside
an adjoining room.
We are separated
by a large glass window.

Round earphones cover my ears
connecting us by computers, and wires:
her work a mystery to me.

I am here to aid
my hearing, to update
my hearing aid.
Tiny microphones buried in my ears
increase sound, an almost invisible wire
attached to a small computer
nestled behind my ear,
a woman's musical voice
tells me when my battery
is running low.

*Do you want a different story? Try reading these words as
metaphors. Choose the most suggestive ones: adjoining
rooms/separated by a large glass window/we are connected, she and
I/sound and mystery buried in my ear.*

She speaks. Interested
in measuring soft and loud.
Is this sound clearer, or this?
Is this volume better,
or this?
I respond until her voice
goes so low all sound stills.
For a long moment I am enveloped in silence.
But I can see her
scanning the computer
as we turn to consonants,
their sharp edges, their blurred endings.
Say cow, she says, say barn, say cone, say come,
say loom, say limb, say let, say lie.
I say them all. Through the glass

I search her eyes for a telltale expression:
She peers over her glasses
and through the glass at me.
My ears are working.
I can hear, I am heard
from my small chair.

She has a good head on her shoulders, my father used to say.

A larger, taller chair.
Another doctor peering
this time into long binoculars,
switching lenses, right eye, left eye.
I am asked to read the alphabet.
My writing tool, cherished letters
that might become
words.

Is this one clearer?
    I see mist, grey fog.
How bout this?
    Better. Black outlines and circles emerge.
And this?
    Yes - b and p, N and M, Q and O differentiate
    separate into neat gleaming parts.
One more lens, one more spin.
And this?
    A Truro sky
    after a long dark rain,
    clear blue, metaphor
    invading description.

I get new glasses.
Distant colors form into
shapes, then faces.
My hearing aids are
upgraded.
Fluid murmurings turn
into consonants, then words.

I wish I had a prescription to see your face
change and shift and I would find a tiny machine
to upgrade my listening, then give you a fresh new battery
to hear my words, a perfect lens to see while I stand quietly
waiting to be seen.

Schubert Sinking In

*"Schubert knew Mozart's and Beethoven's quintets which are quartets with an extra viola. His choice of a second cello as the extra instrument yields new and rich possibilities. . . . The Adagio is the chapter that aspires to the sublime: the serene melody that is gently punctuated by the first violin and second cello; the suddenly ferocious departure into F Minor, with the second cello turned into a deeply disturbing presence; . . . And no less shocking is the Trio of the Scherzo, another descent into the darkness of F Minor, full of echoes of Beethoven's Eroica funeral march. Indeed, plunges into darkness occur literally until the work's very last measure.
. . . The Guarneri Quartet plumbs the depths of this Quintet, one of the richest and emotionally most shattering of all the masterworks in Western music . . ."*
        Michael Steinberg,
        Schubert String Quintet,
        Guarneri Quartet with Leonard Rose,
        BMG Classics.

1.
Fearful and fearless
I go down.
The point is not desire
but the force of unconscious direction.
The music, like an ocean steamer, sways
then moves, then accelerates.
With the ferocious departure
into F Minor, we also depart.
Yes, there are shadows,
silhouettes everywhere, and every
now and then a face,
someone familiar or strange,
someone barely known.
Echoing Beethoven, we plunge
into darkness.
We are shattered.
We have reached
the edge of people dying,
going from our life forever
breaking our hearts
until the very last measure.

2.
Your chosen funeral music
penetrates my mind.
Each day I listen closely
as it composes me
through mourning,
and persistent memory,
and inescapable reality.

And I am trying to comprehend
the sublime, the unexpected
cello, the gentle melody, the harmony.
I lean too much toward sorrow and ferocity
even without a year of loss
like this one past for me.
The viola's punctuated dance
around the second cello's deep serenity
makes it possible to feel
the hope of peace, the chance of hope,
though laced with grief or disbelief.
(For the hope is slim
that the spirit does survive
all on its melodious own,
like the strains of the violins
in the movement called *Adagio.)*

3.
Re-entering the world:
A novelist writing poems.
When is it too condensed? Are prose rhythms in certain parts
acceptable? Do I need more separations, I mean on the page.
Is there something that can stand for something else when something
else is too revealing and might hurt other peoples' feelings?
How do I re-enter the world with all this baggage? When I was a
child I called this heaviness "the suitcase feeling" as if I'd been
carrying heavy suitcases all day.
Why do some of us write our stories over and over, write of each
other again and again, of what we make of the world, trying for ever
more resonant accuracy? Why must we make the colossal effort to
find language for our anguish, our anger, our love? Is our love
enough to move you? Does our anger frighten you away? Is our
anguish sufficient to make you weep?

Would it be better if, even at my age, I returned to the classroom, as a student again, to learn more about the French Symbolists, the classic Greek poets, T.S. Eliot, the language of post-structural criticism? And languages: Hebrew, Latin, work on my Spanish for ordinary life on the streets of our cities, on my French for another trip to Paris some day?
Or will the poems be sufficient fare to board the train that in each new dream heads home?

Re-entering the world:
The war is raging.
My sons are too old for a draft that threatened my own contemporaries – Vietnam then, Iraq, Afghanistan - so it may be the selfishness of the mere witness that causes me to hope a draft, if nothing else, might end the carnage in cities once remote, like Phnom Penh was once, and even Saigon, then Fallujah, even Baghdad, now cities and villages of Syria. The escalating, splitting into disparate hatreds of war. Empathy has become an enormous ocean net. It sinks down, rolls out among the waves, gathers everything in. Unlike cancer, it does not obliterate distinctive function and shape. On the contrary: it keeps each tragedy, each monstrous loss, each brutal or evil human act perfectly separate. Preserves the terrible individuality of every victim's face – a father stumbling forward amid the burnt rubble of a Baghdad market holding the graceful body of his dead child in his arms – dark eyes wide and horrified – *What is this? What meaning or sense is left?*

The threat of meaning utterly lost is everywhere. It seeps in. The young Sean Bell shot fifty times in a Queens parking lot, a memory and now a crowd of martyred dead, more Black and brown sons are shot – often unthreatening, unarmed. My sons, young Black men whose beautiful jaw lines and soft lips, whose gentle eyes and minds might have been his, have returned to their homes safely tonight. But one of them was on the outskirts of a street battle recently, police and other men with guns. Two men shot. Many arrests. Helicopters buzzed the sky above my block all night, my son said. Someone else's son has his head chopped off in the Iraqi desert. I try not to keep thinking the name that will forever sear into his mother's and father's dreams.

A woman in Afghanistan was taken to the town square,
forced to kneel, and
killed by a barrage of stones.
Accused of adultery

I think – or was she raped?
Had she merely unveiled herself,
shown her face
to the rain, or the sun of an ordinary day
of ordinary terror?
I try to resist
imagining her pain –
the slow, brutal dying,
flesh bruised and broken
by stone after stone
until head cracks, or face,
or eyes fill with blood -
I want to turn away
in sinful relief. Even writing of it
here is a kind of escape.

4.
"In poetry, one descends vertically, as into a deep cave, examining
the descent itself, the fears. We are the cavers, descending with
flashlights attached to our helmets. Everything we pass is a wonder
of sudden illumination, shape and design suddenly revealed, then
gone."

Vertically, head down
and heading down
I find the inscription
etched so deeply into psychic stone
there is no hope of erasure –
the truth I have sought
to evade all my life:
Surrounded by love,
we are
alone
and not alone.

5.
". . . brooding on what Wallace Stevens once called the 'handbook
of heartbreak' – the compendium of losses one necessarily
encounters in even the sunniest life – modern and postmodern poets
have even in the midst of (or in defiance of) deepest sorrow
composed countless stirring 'inventions of farewell' . . ."

An invention of farewell
to hope that something
will follow,
that sublimation is possible,
a sublime imperfect
substitution. An unexpected cello,
its alto low and reassuring
beneath the slowly balancing strings.

April, 2006

September Sketch

Her chest is flat and scarred
and there are no familiar breasts
to love and hate, intimations
of a boy's delicate touch, a man's weight,
a hungry infant clinging to its nipple -
that sucking sound.

His cries would soften, then suddenly cease
as his belly filled, taking me in.

Her hips and thighs,
her belly, ass and vagina
all look normal. I think this as I draw.
But how to draw those flattened planes?
Her chest looks dressed in a seamed flesh-sweater,
tight yet creased.

I cannot get her to look naked,
I don't know where to begin.

Wanting Silence

If I remember to remember
let it be without words, let it all be mist, like vapor
on a car window
gathering to blind you
to the road ahead –
just itself, the vapor
like grey silk,
like liquid delicate foam
on a sea calming itself
after a storm.

If I remember
to remember
in the car I will be
surrounded by night
and the darkness inside
will enhance silence
so I will be silent, and sad
as I watch my husband
open the windows to let in the air

enough to clear the vapor
so he can see the road
(well, he is the driver)
I don't want to see.

FLOODS AND DRAINS

1. Hurricane Irene

Predicted for days
Twenty-four hour coverage.
Floods came at night,
with the thunder.
Loud rumbling warnings, an electric sky.
In my neighborhood, rains poured.
We were spared overflowing waters,
while houses became lakes in Staten Island,
roads rushing rivers in Vermont.
Here, only my terrace flooded, water
sloshing over sides, drains overwhelmed
unable to do their work.
There is no drain large enough
to absorb these waters.
I try words extended to pages, but the old pipes
are rusted with wear and neglect.
And no companionship seems to suffice.

I lie down in the middle of day.
Perhaps now the waters will drain
more easily. My thoughts evaporate
in a flash, flash floods carry them away.
Why did I come into this room?
What was I going to say?

My aunt Irene died
soon after she lost her mind.
No more memories to keep it in place,
its interiors no longer familiar
except in shifting shadows
she was too far away to find
her - perhaps a flood
of emptiness – the waters had fractured,
splintered all that was familiar,
sunken, drowned, confused old cries.
A hurricane of liquid disasters,
til little was left of her life.

2. Primary Process

It is said even dreams
are translations.
We make up stories
to hang onto reason,
so we might understand,
through these clever narratives,
  – who knows what?
Old raw feeling, inchoate imagery?
Only the ruthless un-conscious. Primary
Primary, primary process.

3. Hospital Life

My body was immobile, I could not move it
with ordinary intention for days
of pain, I had lost faith
in healing, in the passing of time.

Stiff and made more stiff
by wariness and fear
it was moved by strange hands -
unattached to bodies -
I closed my eyes.

I was moved, lifted, turned
and I was my body, not some body
not no body, not only body
not separate from my body
as I have often been.
I was only myself
in my body then,
my body, my body in pain.

And just when it was most objectified,
handled competently by strangers,
injected, turned and lifted
invaded by touch and tube,
made black and blue with IV needles –
when I saw where it was torn

apart by slender sharpened knives,
then stitched – no stapled! – together again –
the same staples I might use to collect
pages of a manuscript in an old file.

Just when
one clumsy or resentful or exhausted nurse,
or aide pushed, or jerked
or frowned her disdain
at my cry of pain –
meant to be silent
instead loud and full-bodied
angry, ashamed,

Just then
the body remembered its life,
its grace, and *I am alive in here,
alone at last inside* - and
beneath the stiff white sheets -
I stroked its broken parts,
with my own embodied hands,
and traced the jagged narrow hill
breast bone to waist.

As I traced the line of pain
that spread out from that delicate
bloodied stapled scarred hurt place
my fingers touched my fingers
and in my unbelieving way
I prayed.

4. Radiation Therapy

Across the wall and ceilings
Streaks of bright red and green
Lights beaming just past my vision.

I am cold and exposed on a table
My chest covered by a thin towel
My arms are raised in the right position.

I am still and scared and stiffening
Large objects are moving around me.
X-rays, and measurements, pointing.

Two women, young and efficient,
Come in every so often –
They give me news, and timing.

Just as I think I can bear it no longer
Deep breathing to calm my spirit
Both lovely nurses, arms outstretched, come over.

They lift me up so I'm seated.
They return the thin gown to my shoulders.
You're finished, it's over, they say,

And no, you can't see radiation,
The green and red lights only measure.
Streak across air and beautiful faces.

In Japan that year people flee radiation.
Their water and milk are poisoned.
Twelve miles or fifty marks safety.

But this is different, I was told,
This morning when we sat facing
Each other across this vast room.

Now that I'm done, I remember.
I am not lost, buried, or missing, but
I see, as poison clouds move across seas,

A tsunami and an earthquake
Have taken my old life from me.

5. Boarding Pass/ July

A Break in Treatment Schedule:
White blood cell count dangerously low so I miss a treatment
and can fly to Los Angeles to visit my son.

A year full of trauma and terror
I want to erase in an instant
Yet every so often I realize
This year too is my life.

Timing is woven by memory
Experience coming and going
Lost and recovered endlessly
Slowed to an old silent crawling
Then shot like a bullet to death.

Two shots of Neupogen save me
A temporary shield for infection
It will now only lurk at the borders
Promising and threatening at once.

Like waiting in this sparkling terminal
Its shops full of new possibilities
Crystal white lights nearly blinding
As always I've come way too early
Hours before boarding and leaving.

I clutch my boarding pass tightly
It wrinkles from sweat in my fingers
I want to pass the time quickly
Not thinking of life itself passing
I want to be in flight.

Then in my turn to be x-rayed
Plastic cones show where my
Breasts were. Do they imagine
I'm hiding, beneath these shapely
New moldings, a bomb or a gun or a knife?

On the plane I am counting time zones
Changing and shifting around me,
The way to make it pass swiftly
Or stop it to relive the feelings
Is to focus on each passing minute,
Its seconds as sacred as life.

Even at home in my own bed
Surrounded by white sheets and pillows
The best way to get through some nights
Is to read poems and then dare to write.

6. Notes Toward Future Coherence:

People starving in Somalia, their gaunt dark faces, their dried lips
aching for water, filled the screen. For a mere eight days I was
forbidden water, allowed only a tiny pink sponge to dampen my dry
peeling lips.

Attacks by drones in Afghanistan. I watched the fires rage in what was
once a market place, or long ago a quiet sandy village. I closed my eyes
during the scenes of torture in a television show my husband likes –
British Secret Service, MI5. When they extract the tube from my side
that has drained the incision, it is torture. Suddenly, there is nothing in
the room but pain and the shout from my mouth of my husband's name
finds him where he stands at the foot of the hospital bed, his face
tortured in pain.

Jean, Iliana and Jen: Three lovely nurses take turns coming to poison
me, but first, the Intravenous Genius, who can find the vein and thread
the needle in without excruciating pain, causing silent sobs of shame I
cannot withhold, cannot restrain.

7. (Another possible version of it all)

Waters on my terrace, too full to be drained.
How to be conscious of the unconscious?
Agents and spies, rebels are tortured,
Pleading for death on television, on a fictional
TV series, on actual news reports.
Afghanistan, Libya, Syria, Iraq.
Somalians starve, on television
And on deserted roads
In make shift hospitals.
Haitians die of cholera
On television,
And in refugee camps, in tents

Shaken by the wind, or
Horribly still in the burning sun
Glimmering dangerously on canvas homes.

The lovely nurses torture me
Searching for my blue bruised veins.
My body sheltered by a red cotton blouse,
A tee shirt beneath of daring orange.
A perfect black sweater that holds
Its silky shape.
Perfect triangles of translucent rubber
Make perfectly fake and lovely breasts,
Size B, the size I always wanted,
Not too big or small,
Now I have them. They push out of
Silk, cotton, they shape
My shapeless chest where
Scars make interesting patterns,
Cross each other or
Settle into fading, parallel lines.

This time my stomach is the place
Of harsh storms and hurricanes.
Aunt Irene may be watching me from
Distant days when she gave parties,
If dead people do remember us as
We remember them.

Scars in patterns, coherence in dreams
Memories invading, the original only
An inchoate scream. And old toughened
Longing fills me.
I want something out of my reach.

8.
My granddaughter cuddles beside me.
We are reading a book filled with pictures.
The life of a writer, Charles Dickens:
This is where he got his stories,
From his life, his father, the debtors prison
Common in England then.

We gaze at illustrations,
Beautifully patterned colors.

Her hair and her eyes nearly black.
Her skin tan like her father's
Who once delighted in this book
When he was a boy, mine
To cuddle in pillows beside me,

Covered in pale pink and white,
A quilt in embroidered white cotton,
stitched along edges with delicate thread.
Softer than hard wire used
To stitch up my split open stomach
Sometimes it pierces almost
Through layers of damaged skin.

Another time we're on her coast,
Coasting toward the first night
Of Pesach, the night before Seder
Over gentle waves of near sleep.
She is keeping awake, and
Repeating the ancient words dreamily
In English and then in Hebrew,
A language she does not understand
But is taught how to sound out translations,
To make the hard *ch*, the sharp vowels.
We are reading the Children's Haggadah
Large folded pictures of candles
And food and the Order: She will ask
The Four Questions, even though she is
Only part Jewish, she is quick to remind me –
A Talmudic translation of old foolish rules
We all follow. Why is this night
Different from all other nights?
Mah nishtanah halaylah hazeh?
She knows the words with perfection.

Then I sing her my mother's old song,
Who was dead before she got old
I'll be loving you always
The lyrics preserved with precision
Even now with the floods
I can find them. *Not for just an hour
Not for just a day,*
Words I resurrected
To sing a reminder to my sons,
Her father, her uncle,

My hungry vow repeated,
Not to forget what has shaped us,
In dark as well as in light.

9. The Lovely Nurses come to torture me again.

In the huge tan leather chair.
I lean back, raising the foot rest,
opening and closing my fist,
blue veins must rise to the surface
of my one good lymph node protected arm.
Nurse Jean talks of books and poetry,
Iliana of her child and her night course -
life with no time to rest: *And a husband
too,"* she adds wearily.
Jen tells me the names, in a voice low and quiet,
of the poisons she says will make me all right.

All of it here in my mind now,
a tangle of different worlds, one overlapping another.
like ocean waves without borders.
my children when they were children.
my son's ten-year-old daughter, my father, a young man
and I am a child.

I am back in the tan leather chair
and I must have missed the tears falling
when they threaded the three-pronged needle
into my bruised vein because
someone is stroking my fingers
my husband, my son, my friend
I must have missed the tears falling.
*I'll be loving you always,
darkness my old friend.*

10. A Good Story

Surviving chaos and drowning emotion makes a good story, the
biblical sages and ancient poets tell us, the story will get you through
the dark into some kind of pearly dim light, enough to sense shapes,
outlines, even alterations in color. When I was a girl I was a painter,

and then I was a young woman and I became a writer. Now I fear I have missed my calling. Words come to me in images. Moods in colors. If I were to paint this story, instead of writing myself into and out of prison through the painful grace of words, I could perhaps move with less careful intention. I might be able to touch, unaware of course, that process we call primary. Ancient and infantile, it beckons us back to those earliest moments of awareness – a world, a body outside our own, a face so desired it must, we decide much later, be loved.

Write with your body, she wrote me.
Write from the body, she wrote, the fragmented body.
The broken body.
The scarred body.
The disfigured body.
All grown up and developed,
Then undeveloped again.
You have a lovely figure,
My grandmother used to say
when I complained and wept
I was fat and the boys
wouldn't like me.
Now I am thin. Thin and disfigured,
blessing the silence within.

11. Dream
 My granddaughter has dyed her hair, as I dyed mine after the cancer treatments thinned the white so it merely veiled my aging scalp. You're blond! I shout. I didn't like my hair, she tells me, so I dyed it. I frown and then I see her hair is black again. What happened? I ask. Well, you didn't like it Noni (the name she created for me) so I washed it out, she says. I am touched, and I see it was never permanent, just the kind of dye you can wash out with shampoo.

Writing During CT Scan Number 20

I pull on the robe, look
into the mirror, see me, but
not me, then think if I write
it all down, every moment's alteration,
I may be more me than not me, so
every five minutes as I drink
water, pure and purifier
to counteract the IV inserted
into my vein, I write.

Soon I am on my back riding
in and out of the huge beige tunnel
and a voice with a New York accent
says: Hold your breath.
Breathe.
Breathe in and hold.
Breathe out. Inch by inch
the tunnel takes x-rays
of every delicate organ.
Lungs, stomach, pancreas, kidneys, liver,
each with its own music –
an orchestra of perfect harmony.
The hope that no single
instrument will strike a dangerous
disharmonious chord signaling -
illness and possible death.

You are all finished, the kind nurse
will say and help my old body down
off the table. I will dress again,
be ordinary protected again, clothes
replacing the blue striped gown
never easy to keep closed, and walk out
onto the street, into the winter air,
into the world where I wait
for the axe or grace to fall.

Meanwhile:
the new government
intones
fascist rhetoric, all so familiar

we have seen this before,
exposed to tyrannies
impossible to predict
like cancer recurring
they come again
or are postponed
with curative poisons.

2016:
I have a clear scan again.
2016:
the word
metastasize becomes
the preferred metaphor
for triumphant evils
spreading round the world.

III

FAMILY PORTRAIT: A CYCLE

Vincere (To Win)
After the film by Marco Bellocchio

1.
She is climbing the wire prison fence,
but there is no top to leap over
into free space, no height to jump from
to the ground -
it goes on and on,
up and up and up.

She climbs fast,
with the agility and speed of a monkey.
How does she do it? Like a four legged animal,
yet with the grace and patterned rhythms
of a flying bird.

Her hands and pockets are stuffed
with letters/hundreds of pages of small script
begging/pleading for -
declaring her
love, her need to be
seen, acknowledged: *"I am your wife,
I bore your son. Mi amore."*
War! the people shout in the streets. We want war!
Vinciamo!
  She doesn't care that he's a fascist –
  (the young Mussolini who will become Mussolini
  and she merely Ida, whose body he devoured
  then abandoned her and locked her up.)
  She loves his cruelty.
  She's aroused by his power.
  What did she expect?
  Well, she's crazy.
  She expects nothing.

When the pages are dispersed
floating in the winter wind, the storming squall,
she pauses, clinging to the gate,
hands and feet clutching wire,

and she remains, half way
up - attached
to the wire wall.

2.
I am your mother, I am your sister, I am your child.
- i miei amori – my loves -

This time I am clutching wire.
Outside the prison gate,
a winter storm rains down in exquisite density.
I can't see through
layers of thick snow –
a dark sky –
shadowy trees, delicate lines of bare brown branch.
The gorgeous scene
seeps behind my eyes –
joins with words in that old and cherished way,
it's all inside me now
not only on the screen –
a composition beautifully arranged –
her letters with their tiny script
and mine,
I am
climbing,
I am climbing.

I shape a fence of words
like closely patterned wire mesh,
a boundary, a frame -
imprisoning, protecting -
Keep out: to the intruder.
Keep in: to the incarcerated madwoman –
    (where at least it's safe, not because of the absence of
      madness
      but that the story has a place.)
The inside story's bare and dense at once -
naked and exposed, wildly layered and insane.
    (The imprisoned madwoman is not actually mad
      but certainly deranged.)

Black ink crowds the white
and I am throwing story after story
to all of you, hoping for delivery,
watching each page fall like snow
lovely winged creatures -
white moths drawn to light -
and then to the shining, glistening ground
where they are covered
by swiftly hardening hills of ice.

Climbing the prison gate,
the wired wall
the fence without end
I bow my head like her,
I clutch the wire with my curling feet, my monkey hands -
Climbing I am climbing
We are branded by the same mark
Vincere.

3
But what am I hoping for
at this late date?
Victory? Escape?
Release of the pressing down, it presses down,
that radiant old longing with its sardonic face.

There is no prison, and no war.
I am the ally and the enemy.

Ok, I admit it I am deranged:
Disarranged – without a hat, and tie askew,
And quite insane – that too.
And here is an interesting one:
the French: *de-range: not in place.*
So I add: out of place, displaced,
you see why I love words -
Yet words *are*
like swarming bees,
and *I confess,* like her,
I am only broken by the sources of things.

4.
Sitting in a small
Italian restaurant,
voices loud, doors wide open
to the summer night,
The owner/cook, *Napolitano,* he asserts with a sexy smile -
From the South. When I enter in the tiny space,
between the table and the bar,
he kisses both my cheeks.
We don't know each other's name,
but we know each other's face.

On the paper tablecloth
I draw a woman in burka,
wary, or merely watchful,
she is hidden but not hiding.
I imagine she feels safe,
powerful in her masked disguise.
Unless she herself chooses to remove
the dark cloak,
who can know her?

I have hated the burka –
its humiliating erasure
of body, hair, and even face,
as if she is filth or poison,
I have said in a daring angry tone,
No, I shall throw off this medieval rag!"
Words of a famous Italian writer,
in a famous confrontation
with a famous religious leader, a famous disdainful man.
And she did, she ripped it off.
She bared her face her screaming mouth
shouting unedited words.

Now between the salad and pasta course
I see the woman in burka
is a woman with my eyes:
Self-Portrait in a Safe Mask:
perhaps beneath the thick black folds
I hold a gun or bomb.
Or else I wring my tired aching hands
in some old and half- remembered grief -
and glimpse the desire to bare my face

my voice loud and clear and full -
unmuffled by thick cotton wool –
    (for it is still the case, that *beneath*
    the cotton wool, is hidden a pattern.)

5.
She is only nine years old,
but with the confident voice of a diva.
Suddenly she leaps into the center of the room
and belts it out, loud and throaty like Nina Simone
or Betty Carter.

Fish gotta swim, birds gotta fly
Between stanzas, she performs
a perfect cartwheel -
an air-born summersault -
Singing through a deep, professional bow,
Can't help lovin that man of mine.

Behind the loud and throaty voice
of her nine-year-old great grand
daughter, I hear my mother singing,
my father is smiling and clicking his tongue.
And now this child, sings of her father, my son –
Can't help lovin –

6.
I am writing my father's story
as I near his own death age,
I struggle with each page, after all -
I hardly knew him - I who knew him so well.
    (For what do we dare to know
      about our parents
    until they are safely dead?)

But I am mired/sired by my re-search.
The entire project of research
is a security operation,
like arriving early for a meeting,
paying a bill on time,
making a poem out of all this.

The whole point of language is to find
words for unspoken realms of
feeling and thinking.

I am mired in research,
sired by security operations.
Vincere: also: to overcome, to control
explosions, even seepage.

We can make up
stories out of whole cloth,
be oblique and interesting,
fill our stanzas with vague references so as not to offend.
Is fiction itself a kind of evasion?
Shall I write my father unmasked from memory?
Is there such a thing as memory without imagination?

But is not the whole point of language to find words
for unspoken realms of feeling and . . .
il mio amore – vincere.

Arm Over Arm

>After Walt Whitman's *"Out of The Cradle, Endlessly Rocking"*
>*"My own songs awaked from that hour,*
>*And with them the key, the word up from the waves,*
>*The word of the sweetest song and all songs,*
>*That strong and delicious word which, creeping to my feet,*
>*(Or like some old crone rocking the cradle, swathed in*
>*sweet garments bending aside,)*
>*The sea whisper'd me."*

1.
I think too - and often
like you about the sea –
about all that rocking
inside and outside – my feelings –
rough as anger or mourning –
or gentle as memory of a Rye Beach bay
where on resting rocks we lay
in matching mother and daughter bathing suits -
pink flowers, patterned on the cotton
and behind us growing in the grass,
and before us the waves,
endlessly rocking.

As soon as I dive down and surface
I am calm, I stroke and
float – conscious only
of peace, of moving one arm over
the other arm, breathing and blowing,
blowing and breathing.

On the beach my friend is reading.
She is thinking about words –
in her book, in her notebook,
in the Times crossword puzzle.
She is following clues, finding meaning.
Even my husband, who likes best to sleep in the sand,
is immersed in a book –
He loves a good story,
History or mystery.

But I resist returning
to my new plastic beach chair,
where book and notebook are waiting,
where words are enticing, betraying,
betrayals are loud, storming and foaming,
yet some small leftover promise, beguiling.

I swim more laps.
Tired and calm and blank
I float.

I think too – and often,
like you, about the sea.

2.
Once in the city, when the Village was small
with pink and yellow houses,
there was a blue room.
Its windows opened to trees and stone benches.
The beds were thick and high and sturdy.
The sheets were white and the covers were yellow,
my face was pushed into a soft special pillow,
I made a tiny oval opening for air,
I listened to words drifting in through the doorway
or heard a long ago song, now returning
like waves rising and falling.
I learned about stories and surprising translations,
like the switch of meanings in *truth* and *lie* -
they square danced, changing places.
And I made up theories --
one about tiny creatures
living inside my belly and chest,
calling out orders to make things work -
keep alive! they shouted and whispered,
while I tried to understand and master
the words that would keep me from dying,
from death, death, and death.

I wish I had nests on my window sill
in that old room, like the one in your tree.
I would observe the bird life
closely marking in silent awe
the she-bird who disappeared -
the he-bird left with the goslings

to feed, calling her, calling.
I wish I possessed the poet too,
I would eat his living words alive,
his confident song, his assumption of singing
for the collective, the whole human race.
I remember the calling, the calling,
the ecstatic solace of words,
And somewhere that deeper message:
This is what you are for.

3.
Fifty years pass and more
and again death comes up close and calling,
not like the sea, a quiet inviting,
no, a black nothing, an infinite absence, it wakes me.
Unrefreshed and confused I am rushing
to the table light kept on for such nightmares
to my endless words scrawled in notebooks.
The story of my body broken, while
I watched my friend slowly dying,
when out of grief-ridden waters
I came up, and found poems begin.
I learned possibilities and rhythms,
once again I inched over bridges -
toward words, their meanings and namings,
just as in these years as I'm aging
I have come to love mountains
and all kinds of sea grass
and overgrown gardens of flowers and green herbs.
I notice their flourishing shining,
I notice their fading and drying.
Again, death and death.

I wish I had close trees in season,
and the sea nearby all around me,
no reason to travel to see it,
I'd walk in no matter the weather,
and wait for the call of the wind,
the tides always coming and calling.
I don't want to shrink from deep feeling
but I'm waiting for high tide, a calming
to be rocked by, endlessly rocking,
while white sheets and bathing suit flowers

and resting rocks slide by slowly
replacing bodies decaying
my own body sways with the fearing
of death.

4.
I lose words of precision,
of nearly perfect allusion.
How I loved the spaces between them,
between *not right* and *nearly perfection,*
suggesting beguiling new efforts
while phrases and words swirl around me
like wind   like hail   like snow
searching – if words can search –
for a starting and settling place.
It must be myself who is searching,
but I feel the words are searching,
while I become calm, sweetly tired -
I am blank while I'm feeding something -
perhaps it's the baby birds squawking,
and I
am calling and calling.

You speak of the sweet hell within,
hear your destiny in swirling words,
waves of words like the sea.
But where is that confident faith
in me as a poet/word lover?
Is it that a young human mother
failed to return leaving waves of her story -
a story I'm endlessly losing,
like cradles endlessly rocking?
Or that I'm not a man but an old
mother-grandmother poet
wanting the old crone wisdom
but spun instead by questions.
I want the melodious whisper,
the hissed warning and the reminder –
it is there when I close my eyelids.

The hell within can be hellish,
silent, inaudible, sour and dead.
When words return, the sweetness spreads.

5.
It was always inside me -
some interior lit up dark opening -
on the rock at Rye Beach, resting -
my face in a pillow, listening,
walking and racing and crawling
toward the call where the she-bird sings.

6.
Time slows again, in myself, in the sea,
we are rocking, endlessly rocking,
not to your self-song, that enviable blessing,
but to the calm movement, the breathing and blowing,
arm over arm, and I am in rhythm
with even my small part of things.

Shape Changes

Thoughts After Viewing Matisse

1.
I am drawn to lines
by Matisse exposing his process,
outlining shapes and moving a figure,
both versions alive in the canvas.
Everything envisioned, remaining,
the story of creation over time.
How brave, I'm amazed by his courage,
and I long for my deep concentration,
my ambivalent passion for form.

He was unsure of what he was doing,
how to relate to Cubism,
new forms, new changes in art.
One text said, "it was as if
he was afraid of being Cubist."

A shaft of light becomes a flat green triangle,
grey becomes black when it's put next to white,
a thick black brush stroke was once a shadow,
leaves of a plant have become something else,
some/thing in color in shape in space,
and behind new space of a different shape.
The moving and changing quickens my heartbeat, shifting my sight.

Whether to look at foreground or background,
which is which forms an interesting question.
It makes me smile, evoking analogies.
On some canvases, lines tracing his process
are not erased. They are left to be part of the painting,
as if I were to include in a series of pages
an early draft of a story, or thoughts like these
while a poem is being formed.
Or like a life you are trying to understand – yours, or another's,
and it keeps changing.
Perhaps such a thing is not possible.
Understand is the wrong word.

I am writing my father's story,
a work in very slow progress –
it may be a novel – or perhaps biography
or once again autobiography.
Genre, like shape, sliding slowly,
intriguing confusions, blurred boundaries
as I move through his life.
Shapes changing, stories fading,
in his blue eyes, mirrored revisions.

2.
A river returns to my dreams,
and I walk a bridge across it.
The river is clear and transparent,
I can see the sandy bottom,
like a lucid line of prose,
layers of sediment are visible
if you stop long enough to look down.
It is calm enough to dive into,
if you're brave and can hold your breath
long enough to touch bottom.

Then the river is dark, rough and threatening.
Who would dare enter such waters?
Tossed around by ancient forces
you might get lost forever.
Only if you risk a dive, an arc curved gracefully
like the torsos of Matisse's bathers,
can you find your breath again.

On the bridge I see my father
in all his lines and colors,
blue eyes in a long pale face,
old anger and shame evaporate.
We are face to face.

You think you know the story
til the story suddenly changes,
and no one can tell what changed it –
what force insists on revision,
or lets you know all the not-knowing,
lets you see the process,
what you held onto and what you'd forgotten,
both false and cherished belief.

3.
The Bathers begin with real faces,
but soon become circles and ovals
- skin color we wrongly call white,
the earthy pink of his palette,
its beige undertones visible,
a trace of blue and pale yellow.
Spines are thick, swift and black.
A woman - two parallel curves,
one chasing the other,
a young girl's graceful breasts,
or they might be parentheses,
one of them typed or written in the wrong direction.

Drawn to four panels telling the story -
The Piano Lesson's increasing abstraction,
I walk backwards in the artist's time,
from abstract shapes to recognizable objects,
I want to walk into the patterns,
lean on a black rectangle, lie down
in the triangular light of the sun.

I'm in search of increasing abstraction,
if you can call fiction that veils certain bridges
moving farther from actual memory,
a kind of abstraction,
if there's any such thing as "actual" memory,
or only elaborated layers –
the past growing thicker and thicker,
slow shapings and quick explosions
as we move toward the end of our lives.
From those heady years of raising children
when daily tasks absorbed our fears
of mortality, incomprehensible reality,
to these days now, when a day
without a thought of death is rare,
an hour is welcome,
and a night almost never to be had.

I turn on the bridge, heading backward,
as he moves in more closely.
I don't want to continue this story.
I'm in search of a perfect abstraction.

4.
I nestle into the body
of the man who is aging beside me,
at last more real than imagined.
Now I want to write with stark realism,
like a painter preserving:
A vase in its red vivid light,
a yellow wheat field, each stalk
radiantly individual. A careful self-portrait
each line of my actual face exposed.
My father is back in my life
as he was, as I saw him and heard him,
and smelled him – the scent of his shaving lotion -
comes back as I claim him with words.

5.
The line between self and other,
that well-known prerequisite for sanity,
must occasionally be perfectly broken,
I would paint a dense cloudy mix,
like a morning mist or twilight,
not those clean, clear black lines by Matisse.
I am seeing how lines, shapes and colors
change before you can name them,
the blurring, the shifting, the moving.

6.
Here is the bridge where I'm standing –
A woman attracted to process,
unwilling to conceal or mask story,
giving birth to actual bodies –
stretch lines remaining on skin –
like a story pulled from my memory.
Yet I am also imagining,
trying like others before me
to make up my father's story,
revising, renewing, distorting,
remembering, clarifying, confusing
the boundaries of genre and subject,
researching the story of love.

IV

Music and Words

Long Nook waves at changing tides,
fierce water in a powerful sweep,
yet always in rhythm and I
dread to go in deep – my body
hauled sideways, upside down
I twist and turn and lose
control onto a sharp stone shore.
Regaining balance
on scraped knees, I swear
not to risk the ocean anymore,
cross currents I can no longer bear.

Like the anxiety I feel
at the crescendo of a Beethoven symphony –
the intensity, the gorgeous speeding pace
that hurts my eyes and shortens breath
and I rush home to let
a Schubert adagio or a Mozart quintet
tranquilize and carry me gently
into deep breathing rest.

Yet I write in those cross currents,
navigating clashing depths and speeds,
where desire and intention
collide with sorrow and anxiety
enough to drown me like a crushing sea.
Still, I push through and finally reach
the channel where I stroke in rhythm
through the words, even dangerous
words come easily,
close as my body parts to me.

I am a slow long distance swimmer
in the music, in the sea.
Writing words I love and dream
in the music, in the sea,
I am the composer I would rather be.

Like a Door Opening

Sometimes it feels
like a door closing
as if we are talking
about me leaving you
forever, even if I am
saying, I am not leaving you
ever, I am saying
it feels like a door closing.

But then it feels like a door
opening – to what or where
I don't know, and I rush
for air, and if some wind
blinds me momentarily
I close my eyes,
I do not want to look
into your eyes or away from you,
so I look at the door
then over my shoulder until
as if in ordinary time
I say good-bye.

First, the door I leave half open –
then the one I close tight.
I rush into the street
for air, and though the wind
blinds me momentarily,
and I close my eyes,
I am grateful for the night.

Once White in America

It was 1969 and 1973
both times in early fall

when I first saw your small bodies,
tan and rose,
and fell
in love,
for the second and third time
with a black body, as it is named,

and I became
a black body,
black in a way, I'd say
without shame and some humor
for mine is dark tan
called white,

but I am black
in a cop's hands,
he is pushing, pressing
hard for dope or gun,
black at the end
of a rope or a knife
or a fist,
like Trayvon or Emmett,
or thousands more
at the end of a rope's tight murderous
swing, or black as a baton
splitting my head, shattering
my chest, black as a man

I conjured in words,
my story/myself
like my
body-carrying
boys, sons
> *the silken flesh,*
> *the deep sea eyes*
> *the graceful mouth*

flesh darkening slowly
as they grew into
men, Black
men, body and mind
in this White
White country I write and rewrite.

It is 1863
and 1968
and 2008
and still we wait
for the bodies
to stop
falling, our minds
to settle like still water
like rivers
darkening to rich
olive tan, or dark gold brown
after a storm is long
past and the rich moist silt
surfaces.

I am the carrier
I am the body
who carried them, released
on a river of blood
    fruit, strange and exquisite

I am the tan
woman whose sons are tawny amber
autumn leaf and almond brown
cedar umber spring earth
brown,
whose sons are Black
men

a woman who loves color and knows terror
and hopes words might be
the way to everything.

Birth

An empty storm-threatened
beach, but I see only
its stark beauty as I gaze
at the grey water capped with white,
the damp sand colored dark tan, skin
colors I have long loved – brown
fading to purple-shadowed creases
in necks and waists and tops of thighs.
Now, sea grey turns to navy
blue, for it's a cold and rain filled spring.

Can we say this dream is memory?
Or is it rather labor toward a poem?
A September morning is what it brings
to mind, a long ago rebirth and birth.
A second son, tan skin,
light new born eyes,
darkening by the hour to sea grey,
then brown, gone now the translucent
baby blue for black, blacker
even than his father's eyes.

The more opaque the dark I'm in,
the more I settle into
this soft and narrow place,
opening to increasing light.
Then I descend through open fleshy doors
to bright yet shadowed mysteries,
spreading out, closing in,
known, yet strange each time I write.
Each time an empty open beach,
a sea, a tender calming darkening light.

The Sanctuary of Words

We are all thinking
the same thoughts.
We are all thinking
different thoughts, but
not so different
as animals and rocket ships,
more like vegetables and soup
and, I don't know, maybe
cows and birds
or souls and minds
or hearts and brains.

You spoke early,
full sentences at two,
astounding us with your precocity,
I saw the need I shared
and share with you.
I see by naming them
how layers of feeling and thinking
entwine more like woven fabric
than separate sheets of cloth,
like layers of cake
enrich my mouth
layers of meaning enrich
my vision,
both too rich at times,
making me sick,
mind sick, heart sick.
stomach sick always
close behind.

And so I remember the
dark green fabric
my father layered in thick careful folds
on a long work table,
at Isabel's Fabric Company,
the factory where he worked his last
job before the night his heart
broke for the last time
and in a room alone
he died.

When he died
his mind and heart and endless words
layered invisibly into mine
and only now, years later,
do I form stories and poems,
cutting and pasting them, moving them
and folding them into one large bolt
of cloth. Only now
forty years later, do I dare to begin
to unfold.

And how astonished I am
to discover as I begin to write,
that so many poets
are thinking of layers
fitted and ill-fitted,
neat and disordered,
their words mirror my words
my thoughts of night and light,
like old friends telephone talking
or emailing our dreams,
anxieties, and daily chores
every morning, seeking
the sanctuary of words,
old men and women
remembering our fathers and mothers,
our childhood rooms layered with colors and light.

You spoke early.
I remember your eyes shining
as you spoke your first full sentence –
subject, predicate – all in place.
We are all thinking the same thoughts,
yet, we are as different
as mother and son,
as father and daughter,
as two brothers, two sisters,
with shared history of unmatched stories.

One is open, one guarded -
one talked early, one talked late -
and both can be cruel, and both can be kind,
different and so much the same,
in brains, in shapes, in minds.

Passing Seventy

I dreamed
My father last night.
Or, my father came to me
In a dream:
Two different stories.

Maybe one day
When I am long gone into earth
Or atmosphere, buried or burned,
You will dream me
And in your mind
I will return again alive as life.
But how do the forces
That may be recall
All of our faces
And bodies, how do they
Contain the disembodied
Spirits of us?
How will we be
When we return
To you?

When you are seventy
And I am dispersed
In earth
Or atmosphere
Buried or burned
You will dream me
And I will come to you
In a dream as my father
Came to me. I dreamed
My father last night,
We were both old,

And he knew me
And surprised and pleased
In his unfinished room
Sweetheart! he said,
As I will say to you.

Remembering the Queen Mary
and Seeing it in Long Beach Harbor with Aiyana Grace

My granddaughter was six that spring.
Long ago on a ferry she leaned
into me as shelter from the wind
and lay her cheek against my chest
made soft by layering
of sweater, sweatshirt, cotton, fleece
between us. We circled the harbor
and passed the Queen Mary,
now a hotel, floating in the sea.
But once a mighty liner crossing oceans,
I whispered in her ear,
and how I once walked on those
very decks to see my mother off, away
to Paris. Your great-grandmother,
when she was young, younger
than your father is today.
Her eyes lit up.
That very boat? That one out there?
Yes, I said, that one right there.
And cautious of
forced harmonies,
I nevertheless remember
her head against my chest
made soft by layers
of cotton and fleece,
her black hair blown
like feathery thread
across the gray of the ship
the cool of my cheek –
I can see it now,
the curve of the harbor,
the ship, the sea,
each part of it a floating piece.

Dedications

Civil Wars, for Ruth Sidney Charney

Transferences, for D.B.

Watching Children Play in the Muddy Bay, for my granddaughter, Aiyana Grace

Schubert Sinking In, for Rosario Giattino, in loving memory

Like a Door Opening, for Beverly Gologorsky, and for Dr. Louis Lauro

Once White in America, for my sons, Adam and Khary

Birth, for Khary

The Sanctuary of Words, for Adam

Notes

Page 41: Lines by Rita Dove in, "Her Island," in *Mother Love*, (1995, Norton.)
Page 53: Quotation is from the essay by James Baldwin, "Stranger in the Village," in *Notes of a Native Son, Essays* by James Baldwin. (1955, Beacon Press.)
Page 63: Lines are from Carole Rosenthal, (personal communication)
Page 63: Quotation is from Sandra M. Gilbert, in *Inventions of Farewell, A Book of Elegies*. (2001, Norton.)
Page 75: "darkness my old friend," is a line in *Sounds of Silence*, song by Simon & Garfunkle
Page 76: First line is from Jocelyn Lieu, (personal communication.) Words in second line are from Kimiko Hahn in *The Narrow Road to the Interior (2006,* Norton)
I owe a special debt to Kimiko Hahn for her concept of *Zuihitsu* which first suggested to me a form for writing many of these poems with "a running brush."
Page 82: Words from Chinua Achebe, "The Truth of Fiction," in *Hopes and Impediments, Selected Essays*. (1989, Anchor/Doubleday.)
Page 82: Lines taken from poem by Anne Sexton, "Said The Poet To The Analyst."
Page 83: Words from Oriana Fallaci, in *Interview with History*. (1977, Boston, Houghton-Mifflin.)
Page 84: Words from "A Sketch of the Past," by Virginia Woolf, in *Moments of Being*, (1985, Harvest, HBJ.)
Page 84: Reference to *security operations*, general, from works by Harry Stack Sullivan
Page 98: In "Once White in America," altered lyrics inspired by the song, "Strange Fruit," sung by Billie Holiday.
Page 99: 1863, Emancipation Proclamation; 1968, Voting Rights Act passed; 2008, Barack Obama elected President of United States.

Acknowledgements

"Remembering the Queen Mary," appeared in *Hamilton Stone Review*

"Transferences," appeared in *Room, a Sketchbook for Analytic Action*

"Once White in America," slightly changed, in *Our Black Sons Matter*, Eds. George Yancy, Maria del Guadalupe, Susan Hadley, (2016, Rowman & Littlefield.)

    My ongoing deep gratitude to Hamilton Stone Editions for publishing many fine works. I am honored to be on the list. And especially to Meredith Sue Willis, for her work and generous support in so many ways, to Lou Robinson for her always gorgeous covers, and to Lynda Schor and Carole Rosenthal for their support.

    For repeated, careful readings and edits that always improve my poems, I thank my son, Khary Lazarre-White, Ruth Charney and Miryam Sivan.

    My deepest thanks to Miryam Sivan for her beautiful Introduction, and for years of friendship, its intimacy unbroken by geographical distance.

    No words can express my debt and gratitude to my writing group who at different times and over years read and responded to many drafts of these poems with careful listening and astute editing. Jan Clausen, Farah Griffin, in past years Jocelyn Lieu, and Beverly Gologorsky. A special thank you to Beverly Gologorsky who read the entire manuscript, whose insightful editing matches her brilliant writing, and whose friendship has gotten me through these hard recent years. I thank you all with all my heart.

    I owe a special debt of gratitude to Paul Mariani, poet and friend, who took the time, during a trying and demanding year for us all, to edit and encourage "Virus Time, A Woman's Lament." It is a different and far better poem thanks to his gentle, firm and experienced editing. I am ever grateful for his generosity and for his poetry.

    My son, Adam Lazarre-White, showed me how to improve the music of the poem, "Virus Time," by leading me to classic works of the jazz he loves; he has taught me so much over many years about music and about courage.

    My son, Khary Lazarre-White, has affected my thinking and understanding in countless ways and has enriched my writing with care gleaned from his own deep knowledge of literature and history.

For generous response and years of learning about poetry, its forms and possibilities, its music and rhythms, and for her rare friendship, I thank Sarah Stemp. I am grateful to her as well for her careful and generous help in copy editing this work.

I am indebted in many ways to the insights, courage and talent of the members of my Wednesday workshop, gifted writers, the closest of readers, and dear friends – Phyllis Beren, Josephine Wright and Hattie Myer.

In ways too deep even for words, for her listening, reading and endless encouragement, especially through this difficult year of 2020, I will always be grateful to Delia Battin.

One more time, for my sons, Adam and Khary, you have made life worthwhile and getting through 2020 possible.

For Douglas H. White, as always and in everything, I am so fortunate – for unending love and a lifetime of the deepest friendship I have known.

Praise for Previous Work

The Mother Knot
"A wholly original and important work ... I cannot imagine a woman who would not be moved or a man who would not be enlightened."
Adrienne Rich

Beyond the Whiteness of Whiteness
"An important affirmation of a white woman's love of her Black sons. Jane Lazarre, warrior mom, has crossed over."
Alice Walker

"Through the profoundly human caring of this book; its luminous beauty, passionate authenticity, truth and power ... and through the art through which it is written – we see ... the ways of the Whiteness of Whiteness; and we are challenged, enlarged and enabled..."
Tillie Olsen

". . . I cannot think of another text written by a white woman that is like it, and I cannot imagine one that would address these complex issues with greater lucidity, intelligence and love."
Claire Bond Potter, The New School

The Communist and the Communist's Daughter
"Here in these beautifully written pages, Jane Lazarre invites readers to join her on a difficult journey through memory, history, family and self-discovery. This daughter's story of her father yields insight into our own never ending quest for love, justice and understanding."
Farah Jasmine Griffin, author of *Harlem Nocturne: Women Artists and Progressive Politics During World War Two*

"I found this an intriguing, clear-eyed look at a corner of history, the Communist experience in America, that is usually just righteously condemned – or, occasionally, romanticized. Jane Lazarre's vision of it is more subtle: she lived in this world as a child, and now looks back on it as a thoughtful adult."
Adam Hochschild, author of *Spain In Our Hearts*

"You need not have lived through the Red Scare to appreciate the impact of deeply held politics on the dynamics of family life, the contemporary relevance of Lazarre's story and the lyrical grace with which she tells it."
Letty Cottin Pogrebin, author of *Single Jewish Male Seeking Soul Mate*; founding editor, Ms. Magazine.

Inheritance
"A powerful and poetic narrative that seems to float on a shifting surface of emotion. Memory seems buried or drowned. Yet it breaks through. The novel strengthened my hope that art can stiffen our spines, shape up our thinking and feeling about race. Desire and love are radical and dangerous, and the ongoing effort to write seems like a rescue mission.
Sekou Sundiata, prize winning poet and playwright, *Blessing the Boats*.

". . . through the lives of four families whose fates are interwoven across several generations between slavery and the present. . . unflinching in her depiction of the destructive historical assumptions and taboos on all sides of the racial divide, Lazarre's luminous prose becomes an unsettling and necessary meditation on the messiness of America's shared racial heritage."
Wesley Brown, author of *Darktown Strutters* and *Push Comes to Shove*.

The Powers of Charlotte
"A beautifully written tour de force of a novel in the spirit of Doris Lessing and Margaret Atwood."
American Book Review

Worlds Beyond My Control
". . . a special sort of literary adventure. It has the rich, dense texture of life itself."
Lynne Sharon Schwartz, author of *No Way Out But Through*.

"Julia, a white woman with two Black sons, a writer captivated by language, the novel reveals how love works its sinuous ways ... beautifully written, a beautiful reissue. . ."
Beverly Gologorsky, author of *Can You See The Wind?* and *Every Body Has A Story*.

Some Place Quite Unknown
"... as intimate and urgent as a poem. Lazarre's enraptured and lyrical prose probes, with rigor and dazzling artistry, the deepest places of a woman's heart. A powerful and original work."
Jaime Manrique, author of *Our Lives Are the Rivers*

Wet Earth and Dreams
"Lazarre's voice sustains me through the terror of my own most grievous losses. Her narrative, poetic or musical in its resonance, shows how grief that seemed a wall can become a door."
Jan Clausen, author of *Apples and Oranges* and *Veiled Spill: A Sequence*

"She has it right! Perhaps even workers in the field will learn something ... thank you Jane Lazarre from all of us."
Lucille Clifton, author of *The Terrible Stories*

"... a story bound to move anyone who has ever experienced love or loss."
Publishers Weekly

"A book that cuts close to the bone ... Lazarre's severe honesty is served by a perfected literary style of classical clarity and restraint."
Phillip Lopate, author of *The Art of the Personal Essay*

Jane Lazarre is the author of numerous works, in non-fiction including, *The Communist and the Communist's Daughter; Beyond the Whiteness of Whiteness: Memoir of a White Mother of Black Sons; Wet Earth and Dreams, A Narrative of Grief and Recovery;* and *The Mother Knot* (all Duke University Press); novels include, *Inheritance; Some Place Quite Unknown*; and *Worlds Beyond My Control* (all Hamilton Stone Editions.)

The Mother Knot was published in a Spanish language edition by *Las afueras* of Barcelona as *El nudo materno* in 2018; *The Communist and The Communist's Daughter,* as *El comunista y la hija del comunista,* from Las afueras in 2021. Other works have been widely translated.

Lazarre has won awards for her fiction from the National Endowment for the Arts and the New York Foundation for the Arts. She has taught at The City College of New York, Yale University, and at Eugene Lang College at The New School where she founded and directed the undergraduate writing program for ten years, and was on the Faculty of Writing and Literature for twenty years.

She serves on the Board of Directors of The Brotherhood Sister Sol, a social justice youth development non-profit organization in Harlem, New York.

Breaking Light is Lazarre's first published work of poetry.